Victoria
Puri...

By Rev. Victoria Caroline Britt

Marie,

May your life be a reflection of Mary who chose to sit at the feet of Jesus and worship Him. For only at His feet in sacred, intimate worship will we find peace and hope and assurance that all we can ever ask or think is rewarded as who believe.

Caroline Britt

Worship Him Ministries

Rev. Victoria Caroline Britt
Danville, VA 24541
434-250-5288

AuthorHouse™
1663 Liberty Drive, Suite 200
Bloomington, IN 47403
www.authorhouse.com
Phone: 1-800-839-8640

© 2007 Victoria Caroline Britt

No part of this book may be reproduced, stored in a retrieval system, or transmitted by any means without the written permission of the author.

First published by AuthorHouse 11/14/07

ISBN: 978-4343-4314-7

Printed in the United States of America
Bloomington, Indiana

This book is printed on acid-free paper.

Dedication

I dedicate these works firstly to my dear mother whose inspiration and love for God captivated me as my heart cried out in its' search for fulfillment.

I also would like to dedicate this book to the following:

To my lovely daughter Christy Widdifield Daniel of whom I am thankful to God that her heart's desire is walking in the footsteps of her namesake, Christ;

To my son-in-law Kenneth Daniel, Jr. whose boldness to share Christ with others inspires me;

To my grandchildren Makaila Rayne Lopez-Daniel who is my heart's rejoice;

To my grandson Kenneth Daniel, III who is to me a phoenix risen from the flame and ashes;

To my precious grandson, Hayden Daniel, who is the likeness of Sampson in his boldness and strength.

To my beautiful sister, Kathy Keene Collie who has been my strength, my mentor, my counselor and my guardian angel my entire life.

To my Pastors Bill and Sharon Motley and the Abundant Life World Outreach Ministries who have been my spiritual family.

To my precious friend Karen Walters for being so giving and assisting in the editorial procedures.

And most of all to my wonderful Lord, Jesus Christ, of whom I could do nothing if it were not for His grace, love, and mercy and for the comfort and encouragement of His Holy Spirit.

Thank you for all you are and all you've done in my life.

Rev. Victoria Caroline Britt

Introduction

These writings portray my most precious and intimate talks with God.

It was just before mother passed when she reached out to me to help her regain that closeness with God that she knew so well before she became ill. I wrote for her the poem entitled 'Teach Me How To Love You'. That was the first time mother ever realized my gift and as she read this poem, she wept with tears of thankfulness and made me promise her that I would write more and have them published.

Knowing the end was near for Mom, I sat by her hospital bedside as she slept and I wrote *'Le Femini Sacre' which means Sacred Mother.* She was not in her right mind as cancer had taken over, but I read it to her anyway and told her I loved her as I held her hand in mine. Mother passed a few days afterward.

I only pray that the words of my poetry reach out and touch the lives of you the reader and inspire you to know the beauty and holiness and completeness of receiving the Lord as your personal Savior.

There is nothing more fulfilling than to spend time with your Creator in intimate worship. For "Secret, Sacred, Intimate worship is God's favorite fragrance. It is as the hidden orchid that the Everglades seclude."

Rev. Victoria Caroline Britt

Jewels of Content

His Essence

The Tapestry 3
Seasons 5
Sometimes He's Silent 7
My Lord The Creator 9
Creation's Song 11

Love

The Promise 15
Endless Love 17
Draw Me 19
The Lady and Her Lover 21
Teach Me How To Love You 23
Wedding Blessings 25
Is There Any Fairer? 27
The Wings of A Warrior 29

Forgiveness

Repentant 33
To Be Christ-like 35
Jeweled Crown 37

Peace

- Selah 41
- Awaiting The Rapture 43
- Revelations 45

Holiness

- Called 49
- The Call 51
- Holiness 53
- Dedication 55
- Friendship 57

Wisdom

- Casting Pearls 61
- Think Twice 63
- Cedars of Lebanon 65

Worship

- His Breath 69
- Savior 71
- My Love 73
- To Love You 75
- Once Again 77

Praise

Praise	81
Glorious King	83
Your Love Is Constant	85
Longing	87
Breathless	89
Thank You	91

Sacred Intimacy

Brokenness	95
Auk Bin In De Tine	97
Stillness	99
I Want To Love You	101
No Greater Love	103
Desire	105
Wisdom of the Desert	107

For Mother

Le Femini Sacre'	111
I Now Know Love	113

Finis'

Choices	117

His Essence

*"For who in the heaven
can be compared unto the Lord?
Who among the sons of the mighty
can be likened unto the Lord?"*

Psalm 89:6

The Tapestry

God in His infinite brilliance
In concerto's of His heart's cries
The essence of His spirit pours forth
As the voice of creation replies…
On a tapestry birthing His passion
And emotions flowing in hues
His sacredness mirrored
As man breathe's God's life
He smiles and says 'it is good'…
Yet lacking in all of it's glory
The tapestry not yet fulfilled
The most sacred expression
Remains on the brush
The color of His love yet instilled
As His brush meets the canvas
The artist describes
His emotions in rivers
Of tears for His bride
As golden hues … of woman.

*I know of no other woman
As courageous and spirit-filled.
As my mentor,* **Mrs. Penny Bartee**

*"I will greatly rejoice in the Lord,
my soul shall be joyful in my God:
for he hath clothed me
with the garments of salvation,
he hath covered me
with the robe of righteousness,
as a bridegroom decketh himself
with ornaments,
and as a bride adorneth herself
with her jewels."*

Isaiah 61:10

Seasons

Fragrant hues of Spring unfold
Birds are singing songs untold
Flowers' rainbow-painted glory
Canvassing your wondrous story

Summer Solstice warms my heart
Calling me to be a part
Of the fire that burns within
Radiant glory on my skin

Autumn shades of leaves that drift
Upon the wind of changing rift
Lying golden on the ground
Echoes of your presence 'round.

Winter's haven in your breast.
As I seek a place to rest
From the storms of winter's cold
Love's embers glistening gold.

For my Granddaughter,
Makaila Rayne Lopez-Daniel
May you come to know the beauty
and happiness of being in God's Presence.

*"For the mountains shall depart,
and the hills be removed;
but my kindness
shall not depart from thee,
neither shall the covenant of my peace
be removed."*

Isaiah 54:10

Sometimes He's Silent

Talk to me once again Jesus
Your voice is distant and faint
I listen so closely
Yet your voice is silent
What have I done to this Saint?

Was I disobedient? Where did I stray?
Did I wrong my Lord again today?
My heart is so empty
when you are not there
I am suffering
Don't take your spirit away.

Here I am child, don't ever fear
I promised I'd always be near
Sometimes I'm silent
When I need to hear
You calling my name
so sweet and dear.

For my Grandson Kenneth Daniel, III
Know that God is your strong tower
When the storms of life rage
And that you are His warrior.

*"And I will give thee
the treasures of darkness,
and hidden riches of secret places,
that thou mayest know that I, the Lord,
which call thee by thy name,
am the God of Israel."*

Isaiah 45:3

My Lord, The Creator

Rolling hilltops

Valleys green

Snow tipped mountains

So serene

Splendor

Grandeur

None compare

My Lord, Creator

Genuine

Rare

*"How beautiful upon the mountains
are the feet of him
that bringeth good tidings,
that publisheth peace;
that bringeth good tidings of good,
that publisheth salvation;
that saith unto Zion,
Thy God reigneth!"*

Isaiah 52:7

Creation's Song

*Guide my words
With pen in hand
Stage your orchestrated plan
Mountains reach majestically
As drum rolls deep
In revelry
Drifting clouds
Formed by your word
As the harp sings
angelic chords
Waters rushing crystalline clear
As calming violins
Stage the atmosphere,
Man rises from dust
As life in him you breathe
As gentle fingers dance
on ebony and ivory.*

*"As the deer panteth
for the waterbrook,
so my soul
longeth after you, my God."*

Psalm 42:1

The Promise

I chanced to see a wedding today
As I walked amidst the trees
The couple embracing in a kiss
To seal the vows just made.

As the sun rested behind the trees
And I turned to catch it on film,
I looked through the lens of the camera
And my eyes saw a sweet gentle deer.

Not frightened at all by my presence
Her confidence took me in awe
She spoke to my heart with her tender brown eyes
As I heard my master call.

I heard my bridegroom whisper
As he raises the veil from my face
Let your heart pant for me
As the deer for the brook
Take my hand as l show you the way.

As the sun starts to set 'hind the mountains
reflect on all I have done
seal our love with the kiss of worship
and know that I'll come for you soon.

*For **Eric Whitaker** of Casper, Wyoming*
Moments with you were so inspiring

*"There is a river,
the streams whereof
shall make glad the city of God,
the holy place of the tabernacles
of the most High."*

Psalm 46:4

Endless Love

Rivers of silken prose captivate
Abandoned to your voice
Essence of your sacredness
As whispered sighs of love's choice.

In gentle beckons, your heart cries
Touching bloodstained hands to face
Compassion flows moist in your eyes
Scarlet sins your love erase.

Spirit calls within His soul
Longing hearts hear and take hold
Everlasting, eternity sworn
Endless love in purest form.

This is the Spirit of God
Which I see reflected
In my Precious Pastors
Bill and Sharon Motley
Of Abundant Life World Outreach Church

*"Draw nigh to God,
And he will draw nigh to you."*

James 4:8

Draw Me

Dance with me in the garden my love
Whisper your truths in my ear
Fill my spirit with beautiful words
Wash my soul in your tears.

Tell me how much you love me
Let the angels sing all around
As I worship and praise you
And lift you up high
Draw me closer and deeper to you.

For my precious sister, Kathy Keene Collie.
I love to see you worshipping with
tears of joy streaming softly down your face,
Intimate worship becomes you.

*"Awake, north wind,
and come, south wind!
Blow on my garden,
That its fragrance
may spread abroad,
Let my lover come into his garden
And taste its choice fruits."*

Songs of Solomon 4:16

The Lady and Her Lover

Is that you my love?
Is that your voice I hear?
So soft and gentle in my ear?
Whispering your unending love
From lips as tender as a dove
Words of endearment you bring
Fragrant as the buds of spring
Glorious, beautiful, radiant shades
Of love and joy and hope parade
Fill my heart, embrace me tight
And hold me deep into the night
Until I wake and hear your voice
You my love,
are my heart's rejoice.

*"Teach me thy way, O Lord;
I will walk in thy truth:
Unite my heart to fear thy name.
I will praise thee, O Lord my God,
With all my heart:
And I will glorify thy name
For evermore."*

Psalm 86:11-12

Teach Me How To Love You

Teach me how to love you Lord
Beyond the way I feel
Toward my family and my friends
Please set my heart anew
To love you with unending love
The way you do for me
With sacredness and holy heart
And wholesome purity
Create in me a heart that longs
For what only you can fill
Devotion and endearing words
Which cause my mind to still
To focus upon only you
And who you are to me
Teach my heart to love you Lord
With calm serenity
To know that you are God alone
And my life is kept in you
And there's nothing I could ever face
That you won't see me through.

(Written 12-02-05 for Mother
in her loneliness)

*"For this reason
a man shall leave his father and mother
and be joined to his wife,
and the two shall become one flesh ...
therefore what God has joined together,
let not man separate."*

Matthew 19:5

Wedding Blessings

Brought together, drawn by love
Committed to His Holy Word
Walking hand in hand as one
Guided by His Only Son
Bless and keep them, guide their feet
Guard them from past errs repeat
Join their hearts in unity
Awaken Christ's serenity
Bring them peace and joy unknown
Overflow to others shown
All that you can do through two
When their lives are placed in you.

For my beautiful Daughter and Son-In-Law
Christy Michele Widdifield
& Kenneth W. Daniel, Jr.
December 9, 2005

*"For even the Son of Man
did not come to be served,
but to serve,
and to give His life
a 'ransom for many.'"*

Mark 10:45

Is There Any Fairer

Is there any fairer than my love?
Voice soft as the coo of the turtle dove,
Heart as warm as the sun kissed sand
Gentle as a whisper is your loving hand.
Words as sweet as honey's gold
Ancient truths yet still untold
Mysteries like treasures lost
A love so deep that you paid the cost.

"For he shall give his angels charge over thee, to keep thee in all thy ways."

Psalm 91:11

The Wings Of A Warrior

Spirit of the Archangel Michael
After whom you had so been named
Likened only unto the Creator
'Great warrior' the heaven's proclaim

Mighty in battle and victories won
Against evil in heaven and earth
All for the love and compassion
That was planted in him since birth.

Now you stand amidst this great warrior
Side by side with sword in hand
The great Archangel and Michael
Together carrying out God's great plan.

As Michael fought evil in the heavenlies
You fought demons of your own
Though your flesh and mind could not compete
Still your mind was on the throne
And now your pain and misery
And suffering is all gone
You can praise God with the highest praise
For your battle has been won.

And though our vows were broken, the fragrance still remains
Of the moments we shared and tears that stained
Melodies that grasp the strings of our hearts
That love kept alive though we chose to part.
And though I wasn't there to hold your hand
My prayers and thoughts were unrestrained
You never left my heart nor mind
And your memory will forever remain.
Because for a moment in time we were chosen
To create a blessing of life
An angelic reflection of God's compassion
To keep love's memory alive.

*In loving memory of my husband
Everette Michael Widdifield; 12-06-52 To 8-14-07*

Forgiveness

*"For his anger endureth but a moment;
in his favour is life:
weeping may endure for a night,
but joy cometh in the morning."
Psalm 30:5*

Repentant

*My lips kiss His feet
My tears stream warm
Dried with my hair
As I'm humbled and torn,
Stripped of my sins
Yet still in despair
Blood on my hands
By hatred I've sworn,
As crimson fades
to brilliant white
How can I
Toward my brother,
Do less than what Christ,
Did when He died
On the cross just for me?
Forgive me, my brother
render both of us free.*

*"But God commendeth
his love toward us, in that,
while we were yet sinners,
Christ died for us."*

Romans 5:8

To Be Christ-like

*Forgive us Lord, for we know not
Nor understand the reasons
Things we do and things we say
It comes and goes likes seasons
How can we be more like you
Constant and unchanging
Loving unconditionally
Meek and pure and holy?
Cleanse us from unrighteousness
Refine our hearts like gold
Create in us a heart like yours
For testimonies yet untold.*

*"For as the heaven
is high above the earth,
so great is his mercy toward them
that fear him.
As far as the east is
from the west,
So far hath he removed
our transgressions
From us."*

Psalm 103:11-12

Jeweled Crown

When I wore satan's crown I had treasures
Life was fun and exciting all day
But I didn't know then
I was lost deep in sin
And my life I was throwing away.

I came home late one night from a party
And I heard Mother crying this prayer
Be her shelter dear Lord
when desires rage and soar
Be her strength when err satan calls

Then I heard the call of the Master
As He lifted me out of my sin
He gave me salvation
Through mercy and grace
And said that I was forgiven.

A white robe of holiness covered my sins
So scarlet but now none can see
And a crown made of jewels
With a mansion on high
Simply because He loves me.

Peace

*"The secret of the Lord
is with them that fear him;
and he will shew them
his covenant."*

Psalm 25:14

Selah

*Think on me when all is dark
Dwell on spoken words of heart*

*Linger long into the night
Speaking truths until daylight*

*Words that captivate my soul
Passed from days of ancient old*

*Quietly whispered by His pen
Selah at the verses end*

*Beckons me to view the breadth
Of treasures hidden in its depth.*

*For my Grandson Hayden Daniel
May God reveal unto you
His majestic mysteries and secrets.*

*"See, then that you walk circumspectly,
not as fools but as wise,
redeeming the time,
because the days are evil,
therefore do not be unwise,
but understand what the will of the Lord is."*

Ephesians 5:15-17

Awaiting The Rapture

*My soul can't capture
Nor comprehend the rapture*

*But for eternity
And it's serenity*

*We believe
And receive*

*Allow His sacrifice
To suffice*

*As His Word we embrace
'Til in eternity placed.*

*"To everything there is a season,
a time for every purpose under heaven…"*

Ecclesiastes 3:1

Revelations

Dry seasons without your voice
Time to be silent and still
No need for me to make a choice
Nor ask you for your will
But time to dwell on season's past
Of things that you have taught me
To see the growth and changes
And see where you have brought me
A time to just reflect and rest
But only for a season
To understand all that you've done
Your purposes and reason
For soon I'll need to be prepared
Renewed and strong and ready
For seasons change and it is time
To stand and to be steady
For seasons bring along with them
Storms, trials and tribulations
But as I now lay in your arms
I rest in revelations.

For my precious son
Lloyd Irby
Know I'll always love you, my son
As God will always love
His prodigal son

Holiness

*"And he said,
My presence shall go with thee,
And I will give thee rest."*

Exodus 33:14

Called

Listening, I hear your voice
Set apart because of choice
Quiet, calm, all alone
But for whispers, I have known

Words inspired, heart of pride
Humbled, broken, deep inside
Burning fire, flaming sword
Cutting truths, of your word

Planted deep, within my soul
You are now, in control
Will abandoned, you preside
Now in you, my life I hide

Changed and molded, by your hand
Refined and sent, into the land
Hungry souls, lost and alone
Speak thru me, and lead them home.

*"Search me, O God,
and know my heart;
try me,
and know my thoughts:
And see if there be
Any wicked way in me,
And lead me in the way
Everlasting."*

Psalm 139:23-24

The Call

*He calls to me
Tell of My love
Beckoning me "go"
He speaks
With heart full of sorrow
For those that do not know,
He says to me "go forth"
Before the masses with His Word
And lift my voice and sing aloud
The coming of the Lord.*

*But I just fall down on my knees
And cry…"Lord, who am I?"
That you would choose to speak your word
And tell of your heart's cry?
Can I be even in the least
Like Moses, Joel or Paul?
Though nonetheless I will accept
The honor of "the Call".*

*"O God, thou art my God;
early will I seek thee:
my soul thirsteth for thee,
my flesh longeth for thee
in a dry and thirsty land,
where no water is;
To see thy power and thy glory,
So as I have seen thee in the sanctuary.
Because thy loving-kindness
Is better than life,
My lips shall praise thee."*

Psalm 63:1-3

Holiness

Crystalline waters flow from your fountain
Of love and mercy and grace
Pure as a mountain's spring ushering forth
As You reach to embrace.

Still as the waters calmed for the deer
Silent as stars light the sky
Soft as an orchid kissed by morning's dew
Warm as the tears your eyes cry.

Your Beauty echoes faint whispers
Your sweet lips paint a tapestry of art
Deep as your love that engulfs my soul
Your presence pevades my heart.

I love you Jesus

*"My soul followeth hard after thee:
thy right hand upholdeth me."*

Psalm 63:8

Dedication

*On a cliff overlooking the ocean
Waves echo my name as you call
Here I am Lord
Do as you will
Here's my life,
I give you my all.*

*Though the storm rages on wildly
and the cold wind pierces my skin
I'll call on your name
And you'll lift me up
Here's my life,
As I answer your call.*

*"Greater love hath no man than this,
than to lay down one's life
for his friends."*

John 15:13

Friendship

Will you give your life for me
And will to die for love
Compassion strong as heart is true
That mountains you will move
Render your life in martyrdom
Reaching for one goal
Facing any circumstance
Just to save a soul?
There is no love more greater
Than toward a friend in need
That one would lay down his own life
A friendship true indeed
(as Jesus did for me).

For Stacy Wolfe
May your knowledge and
Understanding of God's Word prosper
Even as your soul prospers.

Wisdom

*"Thou art my hiding place;
thou shalt preserve me from trouble;
thou shalt compass me about
with songs of deliverance."*

Psalm 32:7

Casting Pearls

In the dark and secret place
You alone my sins erase

Separated unto you
Cleansed and broken, I am new

Radiating brilliant light
Open my eyes, give me sight

Mysteries and truths revealed
My name written, I am sealed

Quickened by your touch divine
I am yours and you are mine

Ever changing, growing still
Captivated by your will

Teaching, leading through the night
By your brilliant, guiding light.

To a lost and dying world
Gifts of wisdom, gems and pearls.

"Set your affection on the things above, not on things on the earth."

Colossians 3:2

Think Twice

Before you give into desire
And let the flame burn higher
Don't break my lover's heart again
Remember all His crimson pains
Think Twice

When you look the other way
Once again I pray
Just don't give in
Overcome, you can win
Think Twice

When your feet begin to stray
Don't let temptation have it's way
As you're sinking deep in sand
Take a hold of the masters' hand
Think Twice

His love for you
Is too beautiful to lose
For one touch of sin
Cry out for one touch from Him
Please don't make him cry again
Think twice.

"The righteous will flourish like a palm tree,
They will grow like a cedar of Lebanon;
Planted in the house of the Lord,
They will flourish in the courts of our God,
They will still bear fruit in old age,
They will stay fresh and green,
Proclaiming, "The Lord is upright;
He is my Rock, and there is no
Wickedness in Him."

Psalm 92:12-15

Cedars of Lebanon

Cedars of Lebanon
whisper my name
Carried by the desert wind
Of Jerusalem
Exaltation promised
To His chosen few
Righteous ones will
Reign and rule
Lives He will renew
Standing tall
In strength and might
God proclaims to all
These are my chosen few
Those that aren't will fall.

Thank you mom
For the legacy of the Cedars

Worship

*"God is a Spirit:
and they that worship Him
must worshipHhim
in spirit
and in truth."*

John 4:24

His Breath

Breath delicate as Myrtle's crepe
Light and airy without weight

Presence fragrant as the rose
Velveteen as poets' prose

Love that pours forth from my tongue
When my heart fills with your song

Overflowing, hands upraised
As I offer you my praise

Breathe on me with whispers soft
Make my spirit soar aloft

Joining with you in the air
Splendor nothing can compare.

Inspired by my friend
Eric Whitaker of Casper, Wyoming
His intimacy with God captivates me

*"Lead me in thy truth,
and teach me:
for thou are the God
of my salvation;
on thee
do I wait all the day."*

Psalm 25:5

Savior

Wonderful, savior, merciful friend
Precious redeemer, and only true friend
Counselor, Keeper, Cover my sin
Rescue me from the torment within.

Embrace me now and offer me hope
I've lost my way Lord, I cannot cope.
It's you I praise, you I adore
Make me whole again dear Lord

Intimate Father, loving your own
I in my weakness, bow at your throne
Asking forgiveness, knowing you hear
Cleanse my garments, and store my tears.

Dedicated to
Pastor David Kitchen
Of Indianapolis, Indiana
May the song of your heart
Reach God's throne room

*"I slept but my heart was awake.
Listen! My lover is knocking…
This is my lover, this is my friend."*

Songs of Solomon 5:2,16

My Love

*Restless nights, your voice I hear
Gentle whispers in my ear
Your voice, your words haunt my dreams
And captivate my soul within.
Fragrant with your presence round
Your gentle heart's beat the only sound
Shades of amber and amethyst
Fill the room in ghostly mist
Tears fall softly from my eyes
My love is finally by my side.
Hold me close, embrace me tight
Till your presence fades in the morning light
Intimate moments with you I treasure
Human touch will never measure
My heart has finally found the one
In God's only Anointed Son.*

For Joseph Moses
*For showing me the beauty
Of having a true friend.*

*"My dove in the clefts of the rock,
In the hiding places on the
Mountainside,
Show me your face,
Let me hear your voice;
For your voice is sweet,
And your face is lovely."*

Songs of Solomon 2:14

To Love You

Is it wrong to love you as I do?
To want your warmth
and closeness too?
Intimate moments hand in hand
With you there's no desire for man.

What can man give above God
Than present a form of loves' façade
What desire could my heart seek
That I can't find at Jesus' feet.

For Brian,
One cannot truly love
Until they have known Love

*"Could you not keep watch with me
for one hour?
...the spirit is willing,
but the body is weak."*

Matthew 26:40-41

Once Again

Sin is bittersweet
Yet we taste
And savor it's flavor.
It's thorn pierces
The blood begins to flow
His sacrifice whispers
As we see His tears through our own
With a faint glimpse
Of the stained cross
we fall at His feet
Until we're once again lost
Piercing his wounds
With our thoughtless desires
And plead the throne
To take us higher.

Praise

*"Yea doubtless, and I count all things but loss
for the excellency of the knowledge
of Christ Jesus my Lord:
for whom I have suffered the loss of all things,
and do count them but dung,
that I may win Christ,
And be found in him
Not having mine own righteousness,
Which is of the law,
But that which is through the faith of Christ,
The righteousness which is of
God by faith:
That I may know him,
And the power of his resurrection,
And the fellowship of his sufferings,
Being made conformable unto his death."*

Phillipians 3:8-10

Praise

Songs excelling from my lips
Calls from heart-felt hunger grips
Accessing the throne of God
As He sits with staff and rod
Radiant in His majesty
Reigns and rules o'er you and me
Hearts delight in joy and song
Delivered now from all our wrong
Hearts of hope eternally sing
Praises to our glorious King.

*"I will bow down toward your holy temple
and will praise your name for your love
and your faithfulness,
for you have exalted above all things
your name and your word."*

Psalm 138:2

Glorious King

Angels surrounding your throne
Singing praises all the day long
Alleluia to the King
Let our praises to Him ring
Of his glorious majesty
Awesome Lord so pure and holy
Bowing at His feet of glory
Taken by your wondrous story
Greatness no one can compare
Worship we your thankful heirs.

*"Jesus Christ,
The same yesterday,
Today,
And for ever."*

Hebrews 13:8

Your Love Is Constant

*As hues of Fall blanket the earth
In red and brown and gold
The season changes once again
From soothing warmth to cold
Your teachings here are numerous
But one stands out so clear
Your love is yet unchanging
Your presence always near
Though seasons just like people's lives
Will change from time to time
Your love remains a constant beat
From your heart toward mine.*

*"But now, O Lord, thou art our father,
we are the clay and thou our potter
And we are the work of thy hand."*

Isaiah 64:8

Longing

My heart longs to feel your touch
I yearn to hear you speak
The season of winter has come again
My composition weak
My spirit chilled from lack of warmth
Your words of fire rekindle
Comfort me once more my love
As with a blanket spindled
Repair the broken pieces
Where err and sin destroyed
Mold me dearest potter
Renew my heart with joy
Restore this broken vessel
That time has chipped away
And fill me once again dear lord
Revive me again this day.

*"Let them praise the name of the Lord
For His name alone is excellent."*

Psalm 148:13

Breathless

Your name compared to loveliness
Attempts have long been made
By numerous men and those of great
Stature and acclaim
Some call you Rose of Sharon
With prose of purity
And Lilly of the Valley
Recorded in history
May my attempt to honor
And worship and adore
Be welcomed and accepted
And pleasing all the more
For to me you're an orchid
The Everglades seclude
A Hyacinth upon the wind
A scent one can't elude
A mountainside of daisies
And Heather covered hills
Flocks upon the highlands
You captivate my will
The fragrance of your presence
Perfumes the very air
As summer's mist on petals kissed
I'm breathless when you're near.

For my best friend **Lisa Gladden**
together we have shared the
Joy of the mountain and struggles of the valley.
You are a godsend.

*"It is a good thing to give thanks
Unto the Lord,
And to sing praises
Unto Thy name,
O Most High."*

Psalm 92:1

Thank You

Thank you for your truths divine
Thank you for this day
Thank you for your word instilled
To guide me on my way
Thank you for your mercy
And knowing that you're near
Thank you for your grace my lord
I hold it ever dear
Thank you for unending love
Your son, your spirit too
Thank you for your promises
And blessings daily new
Thank you though above all else
For making me your choice
To share your word and love divine
And speaking through my voice

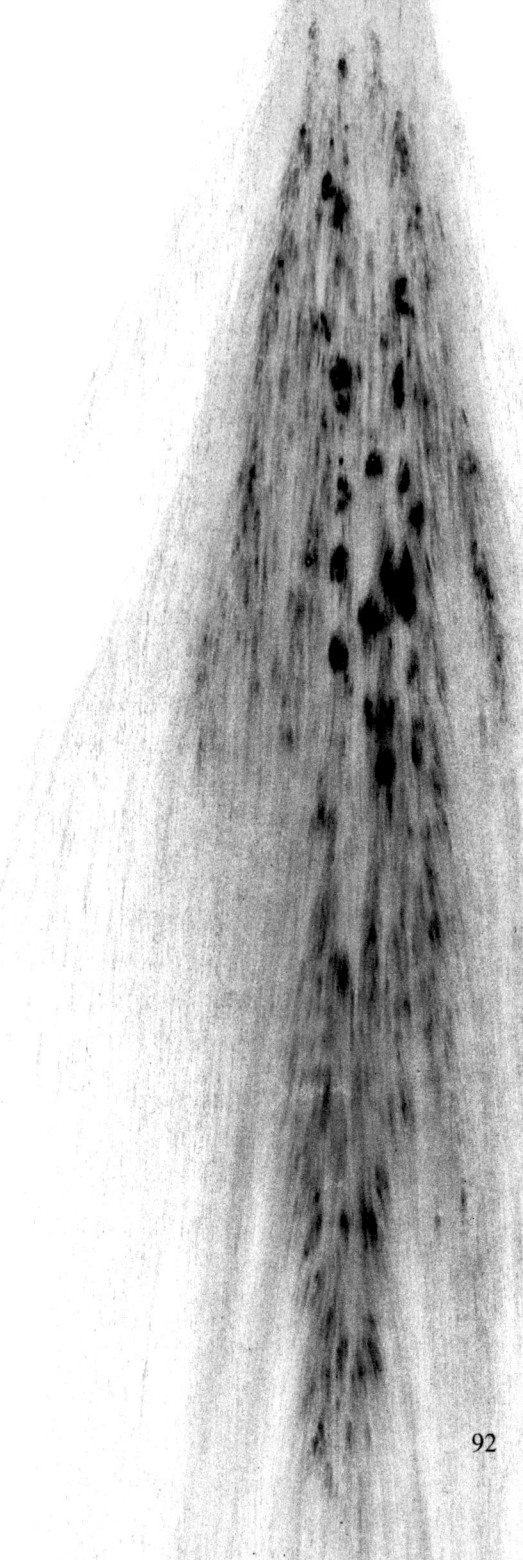

92

Sacred Intimacy

*"He that dwelleth in the secret place
of the most High
shall abide under the shadow
of the Almighty."*

Psalm 91:1

Brokenness

*When all you hold sacred
is torn from your life...
and all that you hold true
is finally stripped away...
as you lay broken
and void of reasoning...
righteousness is born
through the suffering...
hope is born
through the revelation
of the suffering of the Savior.
And as you relate
To His persecution
you die to all but the reality
of the love of God,
the realization of your purpose
and the revelation that...
through it all...
you are Kept.*

*"O God, thou art my God;
early will I seek thee:
my soul thirsteth for thee,
my flesh longeth for thee
in a dry and thirsty land,
where no water is;
To see thy power and thy glory,
so as I have seen thee
in the sanctuary.
Because they loving-kindness
is better than life,
my lips shall praise thee."*

Psalm 63:1-3

Auk Bin In De Tine
"I'm In The Garden"

Misty morn's you whisper
Beckoning my name
Everyone is sleeping
Moon slowly wanes

Hand in hand I listen
Speechless and in awe
Heart fills with your essence
Thru the mist your glory I saw.

Tears warmly trickle
Breathless, speechless and weak
I have been in His presence
In the garden where we meet.

*"Even the Spirit of truth;
whom the world cannot receive,
because it seeth him not,
neither knoweth him:
but ye know him;
for he dwelleth with you,
and shall be in you."*

John 14:17

Stillness

*In the stillness by candle light
My heart swells in your delight
Searching, hungry for truths divine,
Tears flow warm, as God I find
Caught up in the revelry
Glorious serenity
Whispered prayers in passionate pleas
from a heart that's on it's knees,
Captivating whispers sighed
As your face you do not hide
Shining bright within my soul
Soaring as you take control
Still, I'm longing Lord
Always wanting more
To know your heart, your mind, your will
For your voice, I listen still…*

*"Now is my soul troubled;
And what shall I say?
Father, save me
From this hour;
But for this cause
Came I unto this hour."*

John 12:27

I Want To Love You

*I want to love you
And you alone
I want you to be
The only one
That fills my heart
And stills my soul
In times when the flesh
Attempts control
To be just like you
When tempted within
To have the desire
And yet not sin
To turn and see
The love within
The price you paid
Because you loved me.*

*"Greater love hath no man than this,
That a man lay down his life
For his friends."*

John 15:13

No Greater Love

There is no love more greater
And no one can compare
To the love I've found in you
Nor even do I care
To comb the world in search of one
To make my life complete
For I have found my one true love
And no one can compete
Therefore I choose to live my life
Content and quite assured
That no one else can even try
My heart to e'er be lured.

*"And I will bring the blind by a way
that they knew not;
I will lead them in paths
That they have not known:
I will make darkness light before them,
And crooked things straight."
Isaiah 42:16*

Desire

Spirit struggles with the flesh
Obscurity against illumination,
Warring to attain desires
Truth against temptation.
The sacredness of the spirit is shadowed
As the flesh in selfish ragings
Strives to fill it's hunger,
The spirit suffocates in it's aging.
Reaching for the safety of the sacred,
Quiet whispers
For revelation from it's maker.
Why must we have to war
With the sacred and impure
And struggle so to learn
the truth in the heart that burns?
To unite and be filled
With the essence and fragrance
Of the beauty and the calling
of the soul's deepest longing.

Wisdom of the Desert

You have the key
To knowledge and riches
If you know His Word
And His Will

And tho' you trust Him
in the Desert storms
Wisdom whispers
' tie down your camel'

Inspired by my special friend
Joseph Moses
of Dubai, Saudi Arabia

For Mother

Psalm 91

He who dwells in the shelter of the Most High
will rest in the shadow of the Almighty.
I will say of the LORD, "He is my refuge and my fortress,
my God, in whom I trust."
Surely he will save you from the fowler's snare and from
the deadly pestilence.
He will cover you with his feathers, and under his wings
you will find refuge; his faithfulness will be your shield
and rampart. You will not fear the terror of night, nor the
arrow that flies by day, nor the pestilence that stalks in the
darkness, nor the plague that destroys at midday.
A thousand may fall at your side, ten thousand at your right
hand, but it will not come near you.
You will only observe with your eyes and see the
punishment of the wicked.
If you make the Most High your dwelling —
even the LORD, who is my refuge- then no harm will
befall you, no disaster will come near your tent.
For he will command his angels concerning you to guard
you in all your ways; they will lift you up in their hands,
so that you will not strike your foot against a stone.
You will tread upon the lion and the cobra;
you will trample the great lion and the serpent.
"Because he loves me," says the LORD, "I will rescue him;
I will protect him, for he acknowledges my name.
He will call upon me, and I will answer him;
I will be with him in trouble, I will deliver him and
honor him.
With long life will I satisfy him and show him my
salvation."

LE FEMINI SACRE'

(Sacred Mother)

*She walked in a spirit of holiness
Each step carefully taken for God
A sacred reflection of
His mercy and grace
Her desire to live under His blood*

*Though human in nature
And cursed in her flesh
Like Job, her body was tattered
But faith steered her course
As her sails became torn
And like Timothy, she fought a good battle*

*Tears of joy kissed her cheeks
As she thought of the day
She would finally sing 'Sweet Hosannah'
As she took her last breath
And tasted of death
She partook of the honey-kissed manna.*

(Written 11-10-06 for Mother after her passing)

*"He shall cover thee with his feathers,
and under his wings shalt thou trust:
his truth shall be thy shield and buckler."*

Psalm 91:4

I Now Know Love

Time has taken it's toll
Only moments now control
My time is close, but I hold fast
To His promises at last
That my love
Come to my side
Within His wings
I will reside
As he gently sits beside me
And takes my hand tenderly
Looking into my eyes
He slowly rises
Softly touching my face
As my fears He erase
Whispered endearments
Fragrance the moment
His manna on my lips I taste
There's no more time now to waste
To life I can now say goodbye
To soar with Him into the sky
For love came softly
After all this time
I'm with my love
And finally His Bride

A reflection
Of Mother's last moments
On the anniversary of her passing

Finis'

*"This day I call heaven and earth
as witnesses against you
that I have set before you
life and death,
blessings and curses.
Now choose life,
so that you and your children may live
and that you may love the Lord your God,
listen to His voice, and hold fast to Him.
For the Lord is your life,
and He will give you many years
in the land He swore to give to your fathers,
Abraham, Isaac and Jacob."*

Deuteronomy 30:19-20

Choices

Do you know the Savior?
Do you hear His voice?
Do you understand His word?
He's given you a choice.
He said choose ye now this day
Whom that ye shall serve
If you choose to follow Him
Your life He will preserve.
Understanding of His will
He'll open unto you
All that you could ever ask
Or need He'll give that too.
You will never be in want
Nor question if He cares
For once you choose to give your all
He'll make you His own heir.

From The Author

It is my hope that you the reader have enjoyed my writings and have possibly found inspiration to pursue intimate worship. For I have found that this alone is indeed God's favorite fragrance, when He smells the sweet savour of his loved ones offering up true sacrifice of praise and the holy intimacy of their heart's love toward Him.

There is nothing your heart desires that God does not desire to give you and nothing that you cannot achieve through Jesus Christ.

May you all be blessed and enriched and find true rest under the wings of the Almighty God, the richness of salvation through His Son Jesus Christ and true holiness and fellowship with the Holy Spirit.

With love and blessings,

Rev. Victoria Caroline Britt

Coming Soon

With the help of the Holy Spirit, I hope to publish the following books in the near future. Coming soon to a bookstore near you will be:

- ☦ ***A Deer Amongst The Wolves***
  Rev. Britt shares her life of an abusive childhood, abusive relationships, drug addiction, alcoholism and much more, to becoming a minister of the gospel

- ☦ ***The Fruit and The Vine***
  An in-depth look at understanding what Salvation truly means.

- ☦ ***The Keeper of Our Tears***
  When all she had to offer all her life was her tears, God heard her cry. As she hid by an old rock, Jesus became her rock and hiding place.

- ☦ ***Worship, God's Favorite Fragrance***
  From potions to preaching, the Lord taught me that He was the one true living God, the only God worthy of worship.

- ☦ ***Sacrificing Your Isaac***
  Understanding the importance of obedience in tithing, offering, giving, fasting and sacrifice.

Printed in the United States
101290LV00003B/205-252/A